HERMAN'S HIGH-FLYING ADVENTURE:
A SEAGULL'S TALE

DAN LAWRIE
illustrated by Alex Goubar

ISBN: 978-1-989506-83-7

Published in Canada by Pandamonium Publishing House™.
www.pandamoniumpublishing.com

Design: Alex Goubar
Cover Design: Alex Goubar
alexgoubar.com

Dedicated to Kae Lawrie,
who brought Dumbo to life for a
small boy.

Herman S. Gull, Herman for short, was a very special seagull who lived by the sea in Germany with all his different seagull friends; there were common gulls, herring gulls, ring-billed, yellow-legged, and about 40 other types of gulls! Did you know there were so many types of seagulls?

Herman's friends knew he was special and uniquely talented because they had flown with him in stormy weather, and they had seen him in action! No other seagull had this ability, and it was a secret until one fateful day when Herman was caught in a wild storm... but more about that later.

Today, Herman lives in France, but was hatched and grew up in Germany. One day, when Herman and his friends were flying over the German countryside, a gigantic storm that was so strong, it blew them off course and Herman got separated from his friends.

The ferocious storm lasted for two days and when it was finally over, Herman found himself in Southern France!

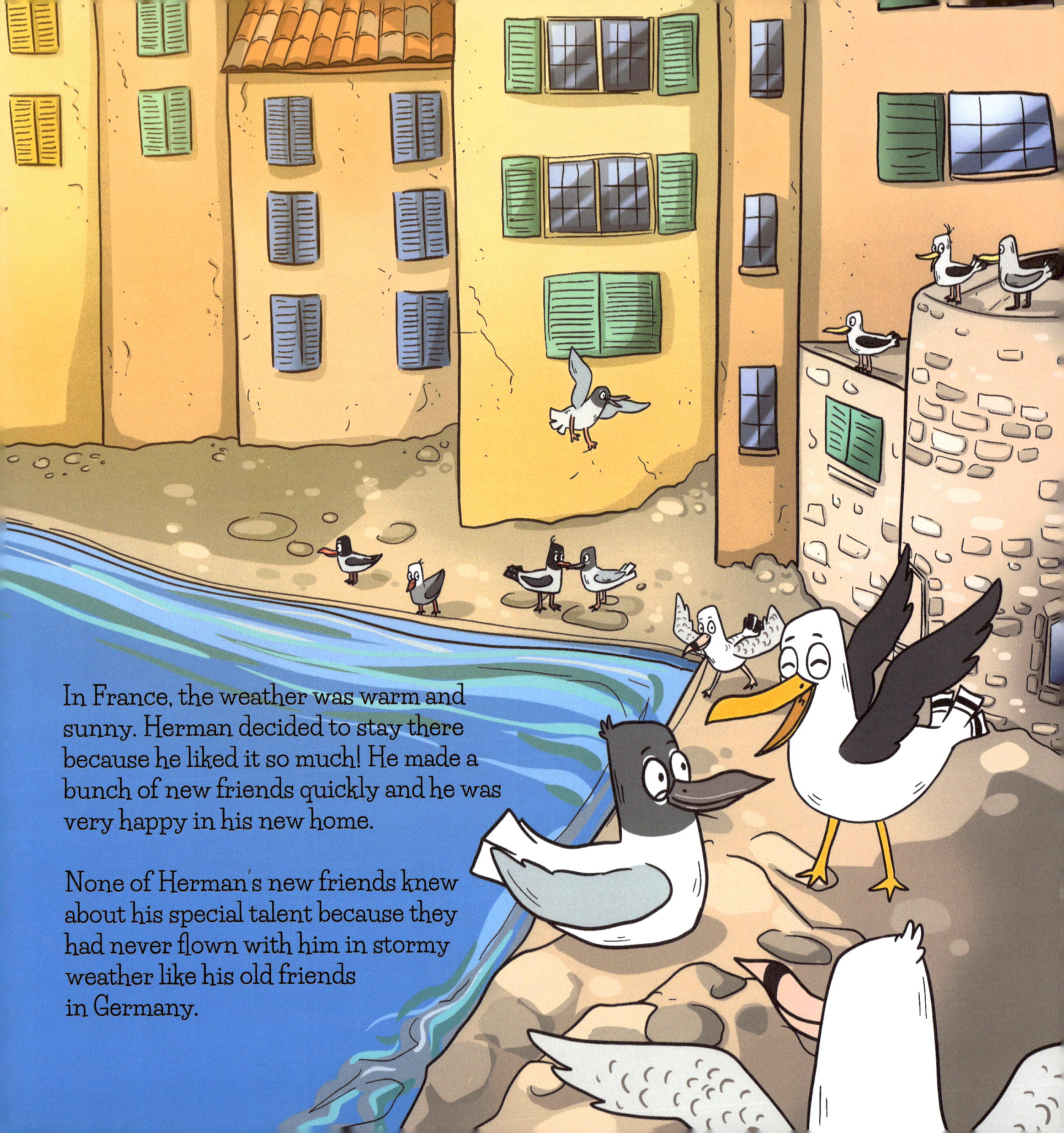

In France, the weather was warm and sunny. Herman decided to stay there because he liked it so much! He made a bunch of new friends quickly and he was very happy in his new home.

None of Herman's new friends knew about his special talent because they had never flown with him in stormy weather like his old friends in Germany.

Most days were sunny and pleasant;
Herman and his friends spent their time
gliding along the seashore, having fun, and looking
for food scraps that were left on the beach. Sometimes people
forgot to clean up before they left for home and leaving
garbage on the beach isn't a very nice thing to do.
Herman and his friends did their best to clean up
the food messes left behind.

Most of the time, Herman and his friends got along well, but sometimes they quarreled over tasty looking scraps. Sometimes people don't like to share, and seagulls are the same! If you've ever walked along a beach, you may have seen seagulls squawking and fighting over food.

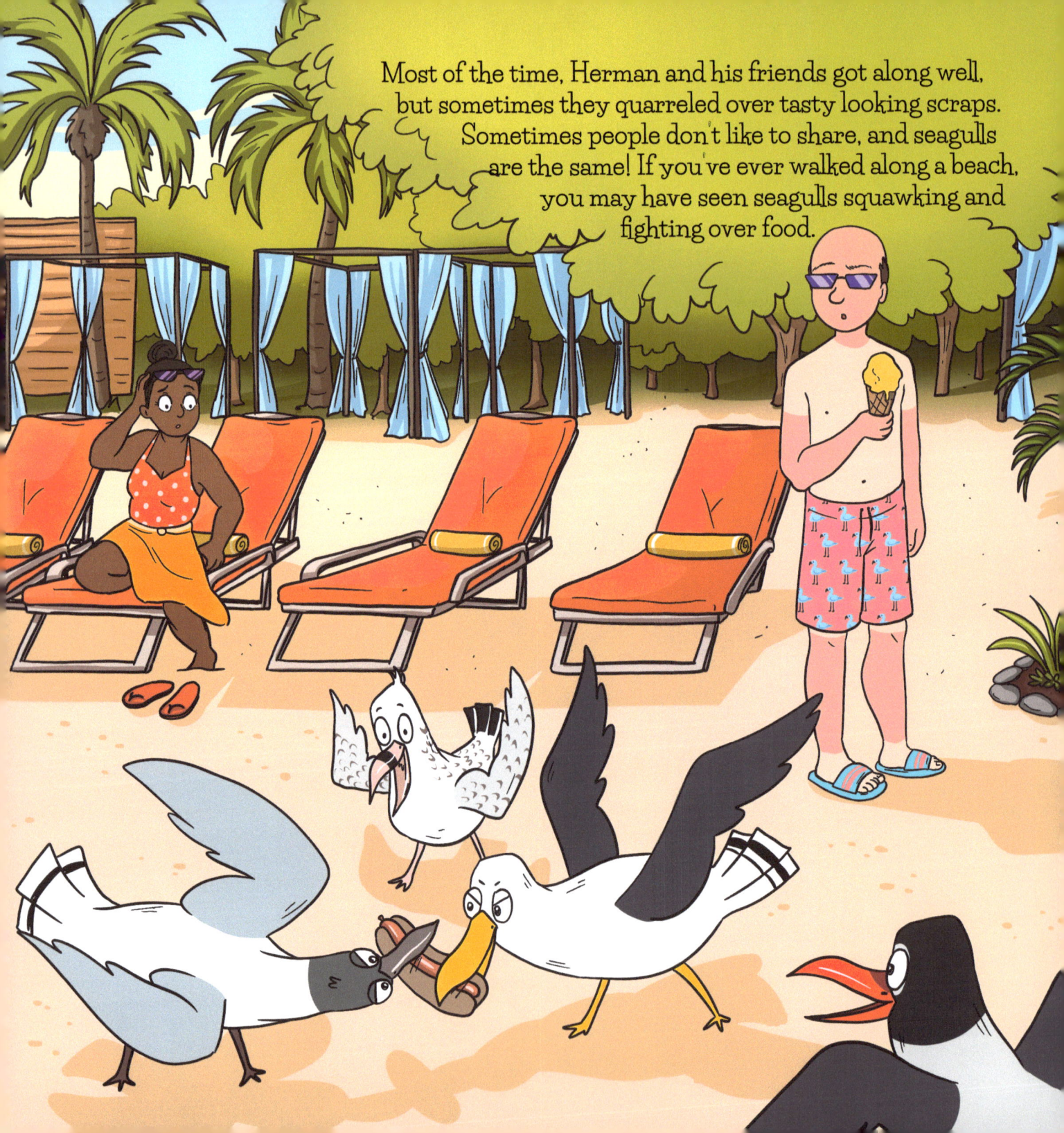

Along the French seashore, calm seas and light breezes were normal, but the weather can change fast, and sometimes big storms occur that can blow in from the sea so quickly, that people and seagulls are often caught by surprise! Herman loved flying on those gusty days when the wind was swirling and howling across the open water creating big waves. Remember, if it weren't for the ferocious winds, Herman would still be in Germany!

Herman's French friends preferred warm, calm days. They didn't like storms and they didn't like the cold! They huddled together to try and stop shivering, while Herman was soaring high in the sky.

Most of the people who went to the seaside beach where Herman lived, were people from nearby towns. They enjoyed cooler breezes at the beach on warm days, and in the summer, when the weather was hot, they were joined by lots of vacationing tourists.

People from all over the world came to Southern France. Some people were from Spain, Portugal, England, The Netherlands, and there were even a few from Canada! The beach was very busy in the summer and there were many languages spoken like French, English, Dutch, Spanish, Portuguese, and German. Seagulls can't talk, so that didn't matter much to them!

One beautiful summer day when everyone was enjoying a day at the beach, the weather changed suddenly. A massive storm blew into the area and people scrambled to pack up their things and rush to their cars; the seagulls huddled together on the beach, but not Herman! He flew into the gusty wind and was soaring high above the water.

The wind was so strong and battered against Herman so hard, that he ended up flying backwards; that's when Herman's unique talent would come to light--he had the ability to speak! No one knows why, but he could only talk when flying backwards, and this often happened in big stormy weather.

Today was certainly one of those times!
The storm was unexpected. On the water, below
Herman, were some boaters from another
country who were visiting France.
They weren't familiar with how quickly
the weather could change and were in a
dangerous situation!

As the storm got bigger, they struggled to control the boat. The waves were enormous, and they worried they wouldn't get back to shore!

That day, a local poet who lived in a cottage by the sea and loved walking along the seashore during storms, was on the beach watching the turbulent clouds, the crashing waves, and the fierce winds. When he looked out to sea and saw the boaters, he knew they were in trouble as he watched the boat bobbing up and down in the big waves. The tourists in the boat didn't know how to get back to shore. The poet watched them and saw that they were looking at a seagull in the sky. They seemed confused.

It looked as though they were trying to listen to the bird! The poet thought he heard the seagull talking to the people, but that's not possible...is it?

I'm happy to tell you that the wind finally calmed down, the boaters got safely to shore, the clouds disappeared, and the sun came out. Herman landed on the beach just in time to see the relieved boaters who were now smiling and laughing at their close call with the mighty waves. And as strange as it sounds, they were sure they had heard a seagull talking to them in a foreign language!

After the storm, the poet went home and wrote a poem. Judge for yourself whether you believe it or not!

HERMAN

THERE ONCE WAS A SEAGULL NAMED HERMAN,
WHO COULD SPEAK FRENCH, ENGLISH,
AND GERMAN, (I HEARD HIM)
BUT FOR HIM TO CONVERSE,
HE HAD TO BE IN REVERSE,
HE JUST COULDN'T TALK FLYING FORWARD,
SO, FORGET IT, IF HERMAN WAS SOARWARD.

ONE DAY AT THE BEACH,
THERE WAS SUCH A BAD STORM,
AND OUT ON THE SEA,
A BOAT SO FORLORN,
THE WAVES WERE SIX FEET,
RAIN FELL LIKE A SHEET,
THE WIND HOWLED AND ROARED,
BUT THIS SEAGULL STILL SOARED,
THO' HE FOUGHT THE WIND BRAVELY,
HE DIPPED RATHER LAMELY,

HIS WINGS FOLDED QUITE SADLY,
AND HE REVERSED RATHER BADLY,
THEN THE BOAT CAME IN SIGHT,
CREW WITH FACES OF FRIGHT,
OF COURSE, AS HERMAN REVERSED,
HE BEGAN TO CONVERSE
(REALLY!)

AND HERMAN KNEW THEY'D BE SAFE,
AND FIND THEIR WAY HOME.
IF ONLY THEY'D FOLLOW, THE DIRECTIONS HE'D SHOWN.
BUT THE BOAT AND ITS CREW,
WERE STILL IN A STEW,
THAT AWFUL DAY, IN THE STORM'S WINDY CLUTCH,
THE PEOPLE ABOARD - COULD ONLY SPEAK DUTCH!

SIGNED,
"THE SEASIDE POET"

The next time you see a seagull flying on a windy, stormy day, listen carefully—you may just hear something you'd never expect...words!

Fun Facts!
Did you know?

1. Berlin is the capital of Germany.

2. Gummy bears are a German invention.

3. The first printed book was in German.

4. Oktoberfest started in Germany.

5. The South of France is known as the French Riviera.

6. The famous Cannes Film Festival is the oldest in the world! Cannes is situated on the Mediterranean Sea.

7. Seagulls can live for 10-15 years... and some have lived for 30 years.

8. A group of seagulls is called a "Colony".

9. Seagulls can fly up to 30 mph.

10. Seagulls can detect food from over 3 miles away because of their impressive sense of smell.

11. Seagulls have excellent memories. They mate for life and form a lifelong bond with their partner.

About the Author

Prior to founding the Lawrie Insurance Group, Dan spent several years in accounting & sales with a mutual fund company, a truck manufacturer and a leading property/casualty insurer. He then became a partner in a life & disability brokerage, where his accounting experience and sales background helped the company become a leading advisory service firm in Hamilton. Seeing a need for a new holistic approach to servicing clients in the property/casualty sector, he created a multi-disciplined insurance & risk management company in 1982, Dan Lawrie Insurance Brokers which later became the Lawrie Insurance Group Inc. that now ranks in the top 5% of independent brokerages in Canada.

Dan is the recipient of many community awards, including recognition as Hamilton's 2016 Citizen of the Year, Burlington Chamber of Commerce –Distinguished Entrepreneur of the Year 2015. Edward C. Bovey Business for the Arts nominee, and recipient of The Incite Award for the Arts. He is the founder and creator of the Dan Lawrie International Sculpture Collection at the Royal Botanical Gardens and has been involved with many public art projects with organizations like the Joseph Brant Museum and the Burlington Performing Arts Centre. He is a strong supporter of Telling Tales. As an active community volunteer, he has served on many committees and boards, including the Hamilton Chamber of Commerce, Better Business Bureau of South Central Ontario, The Burlington Economic Development Committee, Burlington Flood Relief, United Way, The Hamilton Club, Canadian Brokers Network Group and many Insurance Company advisory councils. He is an active Angel Investor and a founding board member of the Angel One Investor Network. Dan holds a Chartered Life Underwriter (CLU) degree, is a Chartered Financial Broker & currently serves on the Board of Directors of the Art Gallery of Burlington. His current project is the creation of the Burlington Waterfront Sculpture Trail.

This is his first children's book.

Alex Goubar is a digital illustrator who has completed her Bachelor's Degree in Illustration at Sheridan College. She had begun her children's book illustrating adventure during her 3rd year co-op, where Lacey invited her to join her team. Alex was born in Minsk, Belarus and is currently living in Ontario, Canada.

www.alexgoubar.com
@goub_art

Flip the book upside-down to
see the Maze's solution!

Follow the red line from
Germany to France!

www.ingramcontent.com/pod-product-compliance
Lightning Source LLC
Chambersburg PA
CBHW042105040426
42448CB00002B/153